CORIOLIS

ارا

**ETEL ADNAN
POETRY SERIES**

Edited by
Hayan Charara and Fady Joudah

CORIOLIS

A. D. LAUREN-ABUNASSAR

The University of Arkansas Press
Fayetteville
2023

978-1-68226-237-5 (paper)
978-1-61075-802-4 (electronic)

27 26 25 24 23   5 4 3 2 1

Manufactured in the United States of America

Designed by Daniel Bertalotto
Cover artwork: *Synthetic Nature 2: #1* (2022) by Sarah Knobel, www.sarahknobel.com

♾ The paper used in this publication meets the minimum requirements of the American National Standard for Permanence of Paper for Printed Library Materials Z39.48-1984.

Library of Congress Cataloging-in-Publication Data

Names: Lauren-Abunassar, A. D., author.
Title: Coriolis / A. D. Lauren-Abunassar.
Description: Fayetteville : The University of Arkansas Press, 2023. |
   Series: Etel Adnan poetry series | Summary: "The Coriolis effect—from
   which A. D. Lauren-Abunassar's Coriolis, winner of the 2023 Etel Adnan
   Poetry Prize, borrows its title—describes a force that deflects a moving
   mass off its course. This concept is at play both formally and psychically
   in this hyperkinetic debut collection, which explores the force of dream,
   prayer, trauma, and acts of belief and disbelief"— Provided by publisher.
Identifiers: LCCN 2023004273 (print) | LCCN 2023004274 (ebook) |
   ISBN 9781682262375 (paperback) | ISBN 9781610758024 (ebook)
Subjects: LCGFT: Poetry.
Classification: LCC PS3612.A93258 C67 2023 (print) |
   LCC PS3612.A93258 (ebook) | DDC 811/.6—dc23/eng/20230203
LC record available at https://lccn.loc.gov/2023004273
LC ebook record available at https://lccn.loc.gov/2023004274

Supported in part by the King Fahd Center for Middle East Studies
at the University of Arkansas.

For my family—born and built.

It was an old theme even for me:
Language cannot do everything

     —Adrienne Rich

Hand me down, give me a place to be

     —Nick Drake

the vanquished search for the vanquished
. . . we deal with a permanent voyage,
the becoming of that which itself had
become

     —Etel Adnan

Coriolis effect: when an inertial force acts on an object in motion and deflects it off course.

CONTENTS

III.

FOREWORD

"What truth is truer than those that start with wanting," ponders A. D. Lauren-Abunassar in the eponymous poem of this eminently curious, lyrical collection. *Coriolis* is a book of wanting, of lack, absence, disintegration, opacity, and yearning. It is a refraction of experience through meticulous contemplation and crystalline imagery. While reading it, we are engaging with a speaker who feels—longing, anger, fear, love—deeply, yet also quietly, observantly. This speaker reveals her interior only in brief glimpses: "I refuse to give up my secrets," Lauren-Abunassar writes. She writes, too, on more than one occasion: "I avoided the question." In this book, trauma, injury, and shame exist in the negative space between lines, between stark and startling images, and questions unspoken and unanswered.

"If only I could cut out the part of me shaped like wanting," writes Lauren-Abunassar. At times, the thing wanted for is love. Other times: family, certainty, belonging, home, safety, wellness, wholeness, or simply for a thing to be clean. Always, these poems reveal the shape of the want by illuminating its outline. In these poems, seeing and knowing are powers possessed by God ("I thought, God knows when to see. I prayed I did also"), and taking them on is both desirable and risky. The power to observe leads to a dangerous self: a self that is capable of harm, one that is aware, and a witness to tragedy and suffering. "What if my eyes were enough to witness something": *Coriolis* is concerned with terrible things, things looked at and then away from, but it consists of beautiful ones, too, offered up by a speaker who notices beauties both great and mundane: "Niagara frozen over in glass"; "A crown pocked with tiny weeds."

"Anything said twice is more true," Lauren-Abunassar writes, and then she proves it: *Coriolis* does its hypnotic work through iteration, repetition, and recurrence. Phrases, words, fragments, and poetic forms return from poem to poem. Titles reappear, and reappear again. To read this collection is to experience the slipperiness of recollection—how every time you revisit a thought, replay a tape, recall a memory, or relive an experience, something is changed. Ideas are transformed, mutated, and altered through repetition. Repetition and revisiting can take you to new territory; in "Reimagining the Interrogation of Betty Hill," the relentless iterative questions posed to a mesmerized alien abductee unravel into a collage of want, first words, silence, hate, and choice. But repetition can result in loss, too: In "Disintegration Loop 2," Lauren-Abunassar takes an existing text—her own poem—and creates a new work by omission in an act of revisiting, a "self-erasure."

This is a book of oblique and obsessive recollections of loss, of withheld secrets and scattered things; of bodies and hope; of places, animals, plants, and seasons; of wanting and lack; of questions; of conversations with God and water and the self. What can deflect an object in motion—whether that thing is a life, or a train of thought, a person, or a poem—off its course? As we move through *Coriolis*, as we ourselves are buffeted and altered by it, transfixed by Lauren-Abunassar's pendulum, what do we discover when we avoid the question?

Leila Chatti

ACKNOWLEDGMENTS

My deepest and enduring gratitude to the editors and readers of the following publications where much of the work in this collection first appeared, often in very different forms or with different titles: *Poetry, Narrative, NECK, Nimrod International Journal of Prose and Poetry, Up the Staircase Quarterly, Palette Poetry, WLA, Nashville Review, Afternoon Visitor, Radar, Boulevard, Newfound, Rattle, Berkeley Poetry Review, American Life in Poetry, Diode, Poetry Society of America, Projector, Frontier Poetry, Comstock Review, Tupelo Quarterly, Datableed, Whale Road Review, Cincinnati Review, The Moth, Zone 3,* and Haymarket Books' *Palestinian Global Anglophone Poetry Anthology.* Thank you for giving me a chance.

Thank you, also, to *Apeiron Review* for publishing my very first poems so many years ago. And to the entire team at the University of Arkansas Press, as well as Fady Joudah and Hayan Charara, for their generosity, wisdom, and faith. Leila Chatti, for not only being a poet hero of mine but also for generously offering her lyricism and brilliance to *Coriolis'* foreword.

Additionally, these poems would have been impossible without the support of PEN America, the Bucknell Seminar for Undergraduate Poets, the Iowa Writers' Workshop, Victoria University, NYU, the Boulevard Emerging Poet Prize, the Palette Emerging Poet Prize, the *Frontier Poetry* New Voices Contest, the Poetry Foundation, Bard College, and Emory University.

I owe a debt of gratitude to the deeply meaningful guidance of so many teachers, humans, and readers along the way, including erica kaufman, Joan Retallack, Phillip B. Williams, Ann Lauterbach, Bradford Morrow, Kevin Young, Elizabeth Willis, James Galvin, Mark Levine, Emily Wilson, K. A. Hays, Deirdre O'Connor, David Winter, Monica Sok, Ilya Kaminsky, Sally Wen Mao, Kyle Dargan, TR Brady, George Abraham, and Noor Hindi. Thank you to the classmates, also, who read endless drafts in workshops and let me learn from their brilliant minds. This includes C. Schmidt, who helped me out of more than one—*actually many*—creative droughts with wisdom and unfailing generosity. Thank you to Ting Ma for getting me up the mountain. And thank you to the family, near and far, who impressed upon me the urgency of storytelling. Teta and Cedo, Stephen and Gracie. Antone and Holly, who taught me to keep going. And as always, since the very beginning, thank you to my brother, Paul. Who I hope to be when I grow up.

Last, my gratitude for Etel Adnan runs back a decade. Adnan indelibly marked my own understanding of poetry and the beauty of asking questions. To receive this honor is more meaningful than I will ever be able to express.

SOMETHING I WROTE DOWN

When the whale is   circling I will be   lying in the bottom of the boat committing
         plagiary: seven   words or more   wondering the water   frozen.

Surviving a heartless   winter feels like elective   surgery: some pain
         I signed up for.   For example, why   not Texas? Or California—Northstate,

driving a road with   no exits   exiting a house   with no doors.   Pressing my face
         to glass. Why not go somewhere   with no coldness.   Why not peer from the edge

of the boat,   say to the whale: I read about you.   Was you, I think
         as a girl who cut   heads off flowers.   Who examined the mud-

bank for tiny.   There is no place where cold   cannot go. Perhaps
         a reason. Small   as it may   be.   A whale changes

the light of an ocean.   Seems to be circling   its own   small reason.
         A whale knows   that stealing is   necessary for proving

one's life is a collection   of activity. Much   like the falling of
         snow. An act   that feels much   like an act. Confessing:

in all my life no one   ever offered   to build me
         a boat.   But why read   into the absence of   offerings? Why not

think of my whale   as *my whale*   to examine or leave   unexamined. I suppose
         there's no kind way   to leave someone,   suppose there's no hold

in a boat. Just   a distance from   water. And life   is that also:
         collections of distance.   Would you believe   this began as

a love note?   Some desperate unclutching   of sound. But of   what and for

whom? I suppose   there is no place   where answers stave

coldness. Suppose   I have lost that false   start. Gone plunging my

hands in confession: It's been years   since I fell in   love with the light

of an ocean.   Since I turned down the sight   of a whale.   Years since I did

some small something   with snow.

I.

ABANDONED SESTINA

I found God in an abandoned laundromat.
I carved the history of coldness on the cold
linoleum floors. Wanted to crawl in the washer.

I said a prayer about the history of laundromats.
The way, when I pray in daylight, God feels cold
and I feel like an unwanted daughter. I wash

my eyes with the history of God showing up uninvited
in dreams. Telling me *I taught you better* in a cold
and God-like voice. Me: crawling into that reprimand.

I cry for the ways I've never heard anything from God
firsthand. Always had words passed down, God floating
like a left-behind sock in a washer. I told my aunt once,

I don't want God to see me in the shower. My aunt said,
God will know when to see, and: *that's*
blasphemous and you're going to hell. I told God, later:

I feel like an abandoned laundromat. Something
that can never clean or be cleaned again. God said
nothing, but the next day I learned the neighbor's daughter

had died after swallowing detergent. I crawled
inside my grief and it felt like a laundromat. Abandoned.
I carved out the history of daughters in my dreams and God

did not show up to stop me. I found this telling
but not telling enough to stop dreaming. Last year,
I made a list of all the laundromats in a fifty-mile

radius. My father said: *what's with all the laundromats?*
I said: what's with the desire to find God, to crawl inside God,
to feel God the way I always feel cold but can never fix it.

In other words: I avoided the question. Last night,
I dreamt I rode my bike to the second laundromat
on my list. I sat on the floor and wondered about the difference

between being dead and being abandoned. I said,
God: have you ever been abandoned? And I knew
this was a stupid question. I searched the floors

for some carved-out history. I prayed to the God
of cold linoleum and wondered if that God
was the same as my God and thought:

that's blasphemous and you're going to hell. I saw
an angel beneath the detergent dispenser and asked
why, sometimes, it hurts so much to believe in something.

She said *that's history,* and crawled into the nearest
washer. When I woke up, it was time for the funeral.
I cleaned my shoes and avoided questions and wondered

if God avoided questions for the same reason I did:
they hurt. I imagined the history of churches
and how unclean they must be. I wondered

what sermons would sound like in laundromats. Eulogies.
In the graveyard, a cold front delayed the grave
digging and I pretended: *she's not dead yet, not dead yet.*

I noticed a little girl abandoned on a nearby bench.
Her buttons looked like angels, her hands looked like angels,
her grief: angels. I thought, God knows when to see. I prayed I did also.

HARVEST

What a season scrubs dry from the young mouth
of another changeling. What Henry calls a shaft of light
falling on the unwashed parquet floors. What others may choose
in those blue hours. There is this, and then: a radio tuned
to the weather station, a weather
tuned to the storm. Some blackberries spilled
where we left them—the heat leaching color from their
sodden bodies. I see a color that was once unbled
and call it you. How long I have tried to clean you up and out
—those state-shaped stains. Outside the reeds march
on like tyrants. Each harvest, they have lived and lost
addled cousins to a breakfast table. And still they keep going,
growing, adamantine. I envy their rooted bodies. I peel back
the hours and search for the light before it scatters.
I open my mouth to pry loose a litany
but all that emerges is a gross tufted cough. Life without you
has not been wholly one thing or another.

DISINTEGRATION LOOP
after William Basinski

      x

Too much like music, this sound. Hard earth becoming

mud earth becoming. Blue whales at midnight. Grief's legibility and then

not. I was expecting more of winter.

What falls apart there.

      x

I hit my head & see blurry. Draw spirals for the doctor one way

then another. I am always involved in this. The tape deck is ripping in. Castoff is hard to pin-

point. To what is owed memorial? My trees never make

noises—knocking, whistling, or otherwise. There are better ways to pass the time.

      x

Static is intentional. The way salmon swim upwards.

Against. Thrashing. Blood in the water, a loosening

knot. This sounds like comfort. The way some part of me

can be found snagged in every nearby tree, roof, post worth climbing.

      x

Rudderless, I sense a small shifting: to every draft a ghost assigned. Tides rush

in. The pain scale only goes up

to ten. There is no space too small to live inside. My ghosts all have ages. There are those

that have been lost in earth too hard to break with steel.

      x

More apparent than fracture: this record. How a voice

can feel like a church. How pith finds its needy fruit

then breaks from it. It's so easy to discern a surrender.

I mostly find life in my dog's eyes. Niagara frozen over in glass.

      x

I remember cut lawns like trimmed bangs.

The skyline as sharpened pencils. I feel light in the absence

of lightness. I stretch out like a sentence & stay there. I think this song, all songs,

are songs about what is left over.

                    x

Grace knows she's queen to the last. Hyssop
is spreading only in dreams. A small dog walks
slow over ice. An irrational number & who uses
this. Hippasus, our garden muse. A crown pocked with tiny weeds.

                    x

Small trees live inside me. This noise becomes that one
& people become people without trying. Suddenly new instruments.
I tend to the fenceline: its tasseled debris. Lose track of
intention. To be is not more than listening.

POEM THAT STARTS WITH THE SOUND OF
ANDY WARHOL EATING A CHEESEBURGER

Rural sound. Sound of all I can do today. Today I thought about dying. Dying seemed like a good idea. Idea is the name I wanted to give my first animal. Animal is the shape of that lie. Lie low said the doctor, just try this. This was supposed to be a poem about cheeseburgers. Cheeseburgers know nothing about dying. Dying seems, some days, like all I can do. Do more, said God. God, I said, I am doing all the light will allow. Allow me to elaborate. Elaborate shapes grow inside. Inside feels like an empty channel water left. Left to my own devices, I would never be able to grow fruit. Fruit is useless in many ways. Ways are all lost and I'm sick of it. It feels like the last good idea up and left. Left, I feel. Feel sideways and wrong ways and gray ways and feel better, said my mother. Mother, I said, the light is dying. Dying is not an idea, said my mother: it's something we do. "Do more."

THE VISITORS

Blue jays ramble my house
like carnivores
      I am barely eaten.

*

Hornets have decided
my sill: a useful limb

skin-like and tempting.
Too hard to hold blood

but hard enough to be
alive. I tell them once,

      I thought you were beautiful.
      What a common story. In the morning

      I shed clumps of hair. I urge a nest and watch

the hours pass,
with still untaken parts.

*

Paul cooks soup on a camping stove while
a wolf hunts the front hall for mice.

Paul, I say, did you hear the bat?
Stuck in the siding, flapping like a fiercely

trapped heart. But this line disgusts me so
I act like a mouse and fling myself

to the wolf who stares. Considering.
          Like the others he keeps going.

Paul locks the knives
in drawers. Slices the onions with spoons.

*

At night, I make room for the deer in the closets.
Just to close the door on them.

To keep them.
I refuse to give up my secrets, but I cry

when they cry. And I say: aren't you tired
of trying to imagine new things

God might have said in the beginning?
Aren't you tired

          of watching for sharks
          in the bathtub?

*

Kindly, blue whales swim
the calm sheets of rain

on the blacktop. Treading nowhere
over and over. *If I grow up,* I tell them:

          I want to be
          more wild than this.

SHADHAVAR

or girl, or wounded girl, or branches grown from
head and spreading—time after time you have
swallowed the hunger, which is to say: yes it's still
spreading—a diligent sandstorm & win wind &
winnow—your saltwhite shoulders & bearable
neck—a memory stuffed into earth & coming up
myrtle, the lesser periwinkle—fresh as a wound,
& an ocean's soft boundaries—like touching
blood means you've touched what caused it—
affect vs. affection—love has to do with the hands
& the mouth—it all feels blue velvet, a little pretty
at first then *too much too much*—you were hungry
& they called you a monster—you found a kitchen
with only bitter apples—wet as the light caught in
your hollow branches—the use of your body is its
humming when windstruck—the same familiar
fear—the dream where they leave you at the gas
station & your basement floods with oil—noon's
small hour & its passage—enough light to bleed
by, enough blood to go on living—haunches sun
stroked fade with time, & darkness has its wild
& wily uses—they harvest your branches & call
you a carnivore—I call you a feeling—or else—
another word

DISINTEGRATION LOOP 2
after William

Too much   sound hard   becoming
Blue whale   legible   ·   and
I was expecting more   .
            there.

            -

Static is   salmon: swim upwards
blood   in   a
knot.   Some
Found   worth.

            -

More   fracture   a voice
can feel   pith   needy
                              surrender
I mostly find life   .   ·   glass.

            -

I   Draw   the doctor
        I am   ripping in. Castoff
            My trees
noises   are better   time.

            -

        small shifting   ghost
tides only go
       to live inside   My
    ages   have been lost

    -

Grace
is   A small dog
          & who uses
    A   tiny weed

    -

Small   inside me.   become
       Suddenly new
I   debris   Lose
                listening.

VICTIM IMPACT STATEMENT

Sent the seedpods floating: viking ships down the river Whispered *pharaoh pharaoh* in my best tree-voice Felt the pallid pockets of earth-traps by root beds and kept looking for bergamot, the coned nose of mangoes Something dripping something halved   The equity of nightfall   Counted Rainfall Felt singular— its each-oxen pat a huffing out the door Called the number to Iceland to listen to melting   Even glaciers have phone lines even Roquefort has its soft tufts of sweet   Caught a hatchling in its pink-skinned phase of barely-breathing and did nothing   Felt free for a second   Dreamt later of its saucer-shaped eyes Poured the good milk out and kept the rotted herbs rooted in their drawers Crushed a dry band of hyacinth forgot to water   Felt power in ushering the drought   Moth dead at the window   Forgot to let out Skirt pooled at the feet Forgot to take in   Took the long walk window-wards Ground looked seltzered with runoff, rain-trail and thick-cold   Outside again and still walking it off Four years fragile and sloughing the requisite thirst   Bent crux of bridgework whispered *London London* falling down by the curb lived an old twisted sap Bore its telling and tidepools or some mimicry of   The river was a dark lung and a fast machine, whistled *humors humors* month-mottled with slow-freeze and soon-enough ice   First there was a mountain then mountains of pale   a series of clocks said *now now*   the moment is for telling   Touched the velour of passing   Felt un-soft for a second A human instant dwindled   My animal eye fixed to other animals   peach pit and roma and what doesn't quite count Histories of dark places etched in   each rock that wants to belong to a river Saw the handbell and rung it Got the mail in my blue shoes—more stars dying Saw the first rat to feast here saw the last bird to go   What if my eyes were enough to witness something

TO WEATHER, WITHOUT ASKING

Without disaster, our car careened to avoid a weasel. Without disaster, we melted twelve coarse white pills in a cloud of warm water & drank. Without disaster, we wore our warmth to Woodstock wed to the idea of weeping while laughing—we hurt for a week. Closed up inside with no dishes for washing. I swallowed an apple whole. You reached in my mouth to see if something would grow. I waited to feel better—the feeling never came.

You said it wasn't fair: I got a body and you got a warning light. When fields would sit wheatless without you. You said some days you felt like Wegener's theory—drifting without your own will. *Imagine living inside the eye,* you said, *imagine the loneliness.* I couldn't imagine you ravaging anything.

I wanted to hold you like a mother, smooth you over and well. I wanted to believe in wolves and the white hours that take them from us. Though I suppose it could be worse—I suppose you could be like some windowless room or the way, out west, they have mostly one shape of you.

Truth is, I'd widow myself to stand in your wail.
It's just an eagerness to find solidarity in misunderstanding. It's just whispering against your hum. It's just a wheaten plum and coming down with wellness and the boy across the river who wants to be a machine.

The whales in the bathtub, the witch in the garden. It's wanting a miracle and getting a weapon. Clearing the white webs from eaves and wiping the fog from the glasses left propped on the washer. It's walking my way to a memory, wondering

over those sounds he made. Like a moth trapped in a glass
of milk.

AUTOBIOGRAPHY AS A HEADLESS GIRL

I therefore learned my hands,
was still dissatisfied. Their shapeless wander

AUTOBIOGRAPHY AS FOG

I wrote about the party dress,
cut clear acres into milk glass.

There is no one I am pretending to be.
This means something

AUTOBIOGRAPHY AS PARTY DRESS

Skin shelved a moment—what makes a party
a party, a dress worth

tearing. There was blood. That was something.
My skirt tried to catch

AUTOBIOGRAPHY AS PENCIL TIP

's nearly indiscernible scratching. When I wrote
about fearing everyone after

it did nothing to nub the tip. Rendered down,
grief is no more than scratching. My fear

has no hardy instruments

AUTOBIOGRAPHY AS HOUSEBOAT

there in the legs: shifting, trying, somewhat
to take somewhere. No longer

blood smeared or dirtied. It washes. In many ways
legless in many ways bodied not—

a houseboat with other plans than sailing
with moving nowhere again and again

men caught at the dock and coming inside
a joke told and sundered

a thing worth sinking. *The pronoun of boats
is she,* he told me. All boats boating towards

her-ness. As if this made
a difference

AUTOBIOGRAPHY AS ERRANT FISH

circling oxygen like a bat on the island
what uses what uses

for light. That age-old question
here always for flinging. I water not.

Nots love me. Not drinking. Not asking. Not watching
for lurkers. Not cupped by a hand rehoming

my hardness—I am memory all over.
I am trying to find my way back to the water.

I am not doing the things they say to do. Not sleeping.
I dream the way I think horses dream:

of running until I starve

AUTOBIOGRAPHY AS THE RIGHT WAY HOME

Housing no findables. Alleys unfilled and not
waking the children. Keep going keep going

my spine my spine. Anything said twice is more
true. Appears in a mirror right before the old woman—

I know her. I call to her. I am her. She saint-prays
on my buckled limbs: lost causes in tendon, those unanswerable

questions. Would have found you anywhere anyway. Was dead
set on the earthquake. Tucking holes in your tiny

joys. As a street walked, I am urging. If you take off your shoes
you won't be able to run. If you don't look behind you you won't be able

to face yourself. See these long nights descending. See these tidal
bones ricked this way then that: a pyre you burn

for the light only. A staving. Off of wholeness
of those first nights after, when you traced your neck for a seam

when you found skin and it surprised you. When your body
was walked down and they said, *Soon you'll forget it*

and your voice drove your body out. Said *You're
okay now, okay*—

CRYPTID POEM

All I want is the bug collector. A matchstick large as a bone—*a bone
has different sizes.* So they tell me. So the long winter goes: sun tessellate, fractal,
soft-thrush insistent. There's a death worm in the closet so I keep the door
closed. Simple. But I feed it, sliding sleeves of lettuce through the cracks. All I want
is something slid back. All I fear is something slid back. All I want is all I fear
and this says something. Simple? Too much so. These days I'm not dreaming much.
Sleep with a soup pot by my head, its white globe iridescent & knocking
at the eyes. When I drive, I leave one wiper pulled up—looks like a cutlass
I don't have to carry, needling fog and the inclement. Every month another
state-sized glacier cleaves. For this, I tally. Hook-shaped carvings on the closet door,
one for every un-dullable noise. World is stiff & loud as an attic: the neighbor-bird's
tapping, the salt thrown outside, loud as the death worm's small
shuffling. *A worm has different meanings.* So they tell me. Simple? Enough to be true.
All I want is a ladle, a box for my bread, a smaller soup pot. As a girl, I was taught
how to fold paper boats just so. *Small enough for a very small body.* So they told me.
Every now and then I try to fold myself to fit the shape. Always easier to greet hunger
with ribbon than with blood. Always easier to say worm than starlight. Bread than weapon.
Angel than shadow. All I want is a new shadow. Old winter shoved in a drawer. A wind at the door
I can mistake for a voice.

HOMILY

Mud miles forward
and stepless river
      bank—on this, imagine
      the moment the moment turned
into a life
      spent waiting for the kitchen to fill
      with mice. For company. For you.
In March,
the wheat got blue and you got
drunker still:
      on imagining the mudflats, the fields
                  where sugar burned.
      Sometimes,
I'll unscrew a light bulb just to see
how I feel in the darker. See,
      in filament, the day you
            pointed to the trees split
            in half from the storm. Saw the color
of a fire's trace then
ran from it.
      Sometimes,
the radio becomes
      a friend I forgot
      to keep or never quite
            forgave. Like the time you found
pills in the junk drawer, tried them
just in case.
It is easy to see
      where the flowers used to growl
      back at autumn, living. Against
      their better judgment. It is easy

to know how this mirrors
                  a finger trying to chase
                                    its way back to the start of you.
                              In July
          the wheat got dead and dying
          to see how dogs feel, you
buried your hands in the dirt.
          You got hungry, after.
          Wondering where we kept the knives.

POST-IMMIGRATION PASTORAL

Remember the one that you loved for?
Giving away all their secrets.

Coarse gray ash
on a coarse green field.

Our father skinning
a goat or pretending to.

Forgetting that love takes
change.

Sometimes I want to say *no*
I'm not finished. As a matter of fact fact

has no matter. Or truth.
Every dream is a little bit jealous

of dying. Every death
is a little relieved.

Remember the two gray trees?
Where the neighbor hung himself

in bundles of wire. And our father
was there to untether him.

For years I dreamt only
of hands. The trees stripped bare

like matchsticks. Coarse
dead body on a coarse live

body. Shouldering him
to the grass. If you could take away

the real things—the pollen sticking to our shirts,
the poplar too pretty to fit,

the lemons wanting
nothing of growing—

I wonder if our father would turn
to a dream. I wonder

who he loved for and left for. Those
widening figs in his hard polished

eyes. Do you remember
asking why he didn't cry then? Do you

remember his steady hands?
How badly we wanted to love, in him,

some unliftable part of ourselves?
These days I ask questions badly.

These days I dream of
moving away.

I'm learning love is an act of mercy.
Love is an act

of sacrifice. Our father untangling
a jacket from a branch.

APHANTASIA

Storm clouds farm the distant field—
is it too late to write about Ophelia?
If I have the look of a desperately drowned
girl? Everywhere people say *good morning*
before the morning has happened. Everywhere
light bulbs are burning out before they should.
Today: the sky is not allowed. Rain can happen.
Hands cannot happen. I lift and unlift the lock.
I try to surprise the neighbors with activity. See:
here she is. Alive. Shocked by attention, I cut
the soles of my feet running to bed. My father:
in the distant field. I see him from the window
looking for the tent that blew away.
He has equally blown some great distance.
To him, there is no such thing as thunder. To me,
it's the thing that lives in the jittery birds. I,
a jittery bird. I count to eleven and feel overwhelmed.
My father is stooping low in the earth like a dream. He couldn't
tell you, now, what home looks like. How did he
get here? So far away. How does he know
this is right? I count to twelve and he disappears. He happens
only sometimes. So far from my wind-heaved stoop.
Consciousness is full of want. Sleep full of want that feels
possible. Maybe the reason my father sleeps through
parties, films, the occasional lapsing car ride. So he can stumble
upon the possible. Today I woke up feeling
like an already said thing. Feeling the cleric howling. My
father: still sleeping. The sky: doomed to happen. The storm
unveils intention & some water falls down. I know this only
by sound: my head most comfortably burrowed.
This sound should be a dream, I think. My father

should be at home in his newly hemmed nightshirt.
Sleep invites the promise that something can be better
left unkept. Love, I pray, is not allowed to sleep.

(21) // VICTIM IMPACT STATEMENT

after Ted Hughes's thirty writing prompts for his daughter Frieda

(30)   Never the varietal and never the wilder berries:
       their new reds look like old blood and I am forgetting

(24)   to open the doors. To close the doors. The light as it were
       looked like razed buildings. I am trying to remember my first flower

(10)   how daffodils come, the hour and its discards. Trying to shave a few more
       moments. I am the welterweight. The slow bloom. The careful breaking

(2)   velocity. Day's perishables. Leaving no scraps. Edging towards wholeness
       before surefit with smallness. Said I miss in each fine detail

(14)   this is the way I miss: clock clicks and foldless blankets, the hedgehog's urchined
       shoulders. Barely discernible noises. I scream to make sure I am still living

(28)   wayward and pruning the light. A small study in smallness. I suddenly
       feel old and true

(26)   like the streetlights' skeletal shadows. In recovery they tell you to draw pictures
       of roses, cars moving down frost-tipped streets, but never faces inside the cars

(4)   existing like remnant. I am the one who survived. I am the chip in the baseboard.
       I am trying to keep the shrubs small and manageably

(20)   whole. They elbow the foxgloves. They ask to be noticed as lively.
       I envy and keep going back

(12)   to the light switch. Its small clicking usher. A stuck point to rival the ceutical
       hedgerows and their various bounty. I cannot fence in and I cannot fence in

(1)   the bare-boned elements. All that is left are the traceable moments,
           the verdure of afterwards thanks to rain during.

(7)   And granted, some crows hunt wounded. Eat their own, stay
           indifferent to rapture

(3)   the necessary changes. The darker ways of sleeping with the curtains closed. In recovering
           they tell you there are no right ways of keeping yourself

(5)   turning. I plant turnips for their white-lilac globes, find they are more earth on pulling,
           have the look of a stern-sunken ship

(9)   and often at night I do not know what to do with this partness. Being left to the washing
           of skin
           in the air and its parity—strange beings outside in the garden

(15)   they do not know what to do with me, their pet: what next, what next? Next we will have
           no use for the new words

(27)   for the each and every window rain. Never the whole river swollen with it
           never just enough but just enough

(18)   stones to unearth from the weedbeds. Distracting distracting. How hard it all was
           to be found here in the mud and its different musics

(13)   when I fell asleep thinking I'd wake up elsewhere. Thinking elsewhere was loam-rich
           with pocket maps and laburnum roots.

(6)   In remembering they say it will feel like the hunting all over. Taking hold by the root
           pulling up backwards and washing.

(29)   I imagine forgiveness is quite like the windthrow in old woods. In remembering
           they say wholeness is only the half of it.

FIELD GUIDE AS SONNET

My grandmother splits plums by the river—her thumbs are the thumbs of a god:
they divide, they multiply, they extend. She chews a mint leaf down until it is her own

green-colored spit. And when she smokes, the ash does not fall without her say-
so. So: she is a study in force. How to channel the mighty in her own

lithe hands. I told her once: I don't know how to not be shaped or how to move
beyond this. She said: this is a question of life. Like: *get over it*. Her mercy flows like a clumsy

river. It moves mad and it carries a hazard of surprises. She surprises me
by saying: grief's no more than a postcard in lieu of a letter, a plum where a garden should be,

a disappointment you pull from the root. Look: the onward's in the looking, she says.
To the history of other derailments and the women who tendered their manner of moving

on. She is a woman who knows: pain is no more than a wager on survivability. She dreams
in the language of history. When she eats, she keeps one hand open. When she prays

she requires no answers. Still: when she sleeps, she whispers what I whisper.
I want something for keeps.

II.

AUTOPSY

for Kigali: "a first time mother [who] gave birth to
two cubs Friday before eating them Monday" (CNN)

I remember hitchhiking to Kansas when I was
eighteen. Never once thought of my mother,
sharpening her teeth in the kitchen. Animal:
her ways of preparing. Animal. That traceless center—
the inside of the truck warm
like a pelt of fur, like my mother's shoulderblade:

there in the pitch and roll of highway. Once saw her
milk a bone dry of marrow, smuggle a steak knife
beneath her pillow *in case*—her neck pricked
with tiny mistakes come morning. Once saw my father kneel
bone-tired to lace up her snowshoes. How animal:
her stalky walk. Her keeping. No lions

in Kansas; no mothers either. Just stalks bent earth-
ward. Wheat tipped like mother's next question
how late there, how long there, and why there?
Might as well be a jungle: those weather-scraped
plains. In need of a cyclone to uproot my own
hitchless ribs, my light-left eyes. Each day a study

of my body's unbecoming—my skin more like hers
my mouth more like hers, my hammock of muscles,
her fevers. Fevered, I once saw my mother blow a house
down. Roar life into the body of a cluster of seeds. When caged
she eats daylight. She eats daylight often. She knows
there are rules. *Some mothers eat their young,*

when they sense something's wrong.
Some mothers unravel and never stop unraveling:
the whole story. The midnight call. The confession:

I said no over and over—
and of course it's never *really* a jungle. *I got in a car once too*
she says. And she swallows

my tiny life. My mutiny done once already. Once
I remember her dreaming. Her long body there on a sofa green
like the tops of trees. Jungle fever. Her legs' spasmed urging
like trying to run to her Kansas. Like trying to stalk. Like
moving to swallow each and every wrong thing passed down—
how animals, like Kigali, know a plan and stick to it,

thinking what gets swallowed's what gets kept. Theirs
for defeating. Their wrong for righting, their Kansan
flat walked: where the world gets cageless. Where their children:
cageless. Once I saw my mother watch the light hit
my shoulders. And inside her—animals seeing

in their cages, in their children, in their wanting.
Mistaking the light for leaves

WHERE HAVE YOU GONE, CONNIE CONVERSE

and why am I waiting? To find your shape shaving
light into lines on a blue carpet: gray, hard answers to
where was I, what flowers, how early—

Every day we claim losses not ours. This is not changing.

Granted, each time I pray I say sorry and nothing happens. Furthermore
I've lit plenty of bushes on fire. For all my fond remembering
I've never remembered you exactly.

Who belongs to what is always the question. No matter what they tell you.

But I imagine that knuckle thumbing out, hedging bets on bison
who sweep the snow, turn to face weather ambling: girl-shouldered
and wanting, roving woman, child-bride, growing lily to consider—

When I lace my shoes, I imagine myself fastened to fate. When I cry I see bluebirds.

Granted, you sang some. *How sad, how lovely,* the roving that keep roving
the blue cars that fill and the bodies that don't. Often I imagine a house filled
with tiny rooms. A woman who grows old, rises early.

My blood begs to be an ocean. *My* song is a song about wild things brought in.

MAJOR ARCANA 2: THE INSTRUMENTS
after Frances F. Denny

oxymel jarred
some filament floats,
     some petals press down
in a hue like fresh-welt

angostura & apple &
     daisy chain of wantless stems
the ultimate hedgewitch,
the right side of chiaroscuro

her measurements murmur
     her boiled wings
the blessed uses take the hawk

wing and strip it
     that awful thrashing gives way
grind a fine dust to pale
for the light-left eyes

take the sourceless light and marry
     to pretty clusters of concrete-weeds:
     tiny elbows of wanting

give me a drink & i'll drink it
heave off last trespass
     pepper lung and harden water
     new body new body new body

     weft and warp thread
     thread story to prediction
     to heartache to cure

power no more
than a thumb-traced raincoat
        no pre-caught hawk
        no silent ask

the truth of snared bodies is always
        toe touch to mouth touch to memories of
breath: the body a thing
        the body a tense
        the body a prayer
of its own making

I DROP A WHITE PILL IN MY SINK

& bleed elsewhere one following, ripe month. Finger daggered,
toothbed exposed girl-wet & teasing, my breast tugged away from my chest:
a zippered wound—red red river, overflowing river, appled midnight—moon
a bitten core. Doesn't really matter. My knee skinned to bone. My razored
thigh. Licking the sink side like drinking the snow. Apparently Edna. Apparently
my mother. Apparently I will never be holdable again. Tongue-cut
metal. The whole world metal. The whole world one small paper box. A paper cut
on my earlobe. Thin cut like a toothbrush bristle. Never why. My thighs all-over harsh. Dreams
hard as marl. I cut my feet again and again. On my dreams. I cast my ash in the river. *I earned
this. I walked in Georgia.* If you give a girl an abortion, she's going to ask
for another abortion. So the story goes. A blister presses crisp as a shirt, relinquishes blood
there beneath skin: lagoonal. My private party. My TV turned down. Snow turned
to rain. Body backlit and finally: dripping. Bleeding. The sink is a stilted oracle. She drains. I drain.
Un-weft, I wept. I never told my mother.

REIMAGINING THE INTERROGATION OF BETTY HILL

i.

Have you seen him?

> I've scene-played the whole thing out:
> the just-there eclipse,
>
> the pockmarked car. If I had to pick
> a favorite dress I'd pick moonlight
>
> and not wonder why he stole me

Where do you see him?

> Incidentally, my first word was seaworthy.
> On a day-to-day basis I imagine my beloved
>
> shaped out in gray pipe cleaner:
> his wrist bones are fine as windpipes
>
> but I don't have to breathe him to know
> that he lives for leaf-burdened gutters
>
> and palindromes. The same start as the ending
> comforts him, the slow march of small cursive script.
>
> When I see him he looks like he wants to smooth
> my eyebrows or give me new skin to walk around in,

a blemish on the sole of my right foot, a fat blister
under my thumb, a passport to silent country

where quartz glitters bright as a blood oath. I see him
mostly in car exhaust—breathe deep and ceaseless

And what do you live off of?

The top of my head, but where is the bottom?
I have bottomed all outs, he sneaks quietly through.

He knows about light's shelf life—its briny appeal

What does he say?

Prayers that sound like salad recipes
the antidote to hunger is not eating

but bleeding—& sliced black olives
make the best hoop earrings

That's a good story. Why does he say that?

Because there's no late-night TV in the other dimension
and I'm tired of gimmicks. I never wanted to be the person

who spoke quietly. I never wanted to be afraid of each and every
star—like eraser-torn holes in a blue-black sheet of paper

warm from the printer. I was drawn, did I tell you? That he studied
and bound my each loose turn. My own phantom limb pains

each time he traces my penciled edge—

What are you afraid of?

> Hillsides. The right way home. I have learned my own name,
> I have said my own name. I have buried the sheets that I slept on.
>
> I have slept with the windows unlocked
> and racked each stranger's elbow
>
> for a tiny taste of want

ii.

Can you describe the feeling, Betty, can you?

> Can you describe the feeling
> of a water-filled thirst

Do you remember the sound of his voice?

> I remember it lovely
> and not-supposed-to-be-lovely
>
> like a tongue on an envelope, or
> the first-bitten grape

Was he Khrushchev?

> More like Demikhov screwing
> the heads onto dogs

Was he ecstatic?

> More like the staticky sweater
> I wear each Christmas

Does he control you?

> As a girl I had always been own-less
> I gave away easily
>
> each prayer, each gift. I remember the letter
> my mother sent. I remember the taste of poinsettia.
>
> And I heard what Cassie said about the boy on the bus,
> his fast-colder hands. Who doesn't feel controlled?
>
> Now and then. When he opened the night and reached down
> it could have been a god in his best white-trousers. Could
>
> have been dirt running towards the drain. I felt pulled.
> I feel pulled

Are you small, a very small little girl, or a big person, grown up?

> I am the errant fish, the long-lost harbinger
> I told him everywhere I am soft I am touched
>
> and I hate that. He said:
> where your heart a trumpet is

iii.

What do you feel?

      . . . too much—

Is he a bad guy?

      [SILENCE]

Do you like him?

      [SILENCE]

Do you like bad guys, Betty?

      I like guys good at guise
      I like green doors, not red ones

      I like jars filled with ash,
      temples fit to hold urges

      I like dustpans and stoplights
      the yellow neon of pollen

      on the bottom of everything
      I like water rings and coal heaps

      cellophane pulled tight round my
      ankles like liquid glass. Given a choice

I would eat the choice
I would keep it inside me

The cold thing—where do they put it?

As a girl I held interests in drowning.
Wore my water-walking shoes

to the lake then sunk. Felt the color deepen
as the water deepened

and this is where they put each lost thing. This
is where he put me again, in this moment

with the cold things that used to be warm things
with the hollow bones of birds who tried, like me,

to—

Do you see him?

My first word was seaworthy
my next word was pond

What does he look like?

Like Ike or me trying
to avoid the question

I will not yield the floor. I will not clean the floor.
In all my life I have never held the last word

But what does he look like?

The hypnotist posed over each small life
that claims to be large

the underside of undeveloped photographs
a thin sleeve of *yes yes yes*—

in the room I was given a gown. In the gown
I was given a word. My name

was a tiny bird

EKPHRASTIC POEM OF A HURRICANE HUE PAINT
SWATCH, OR: THINGS THAT ARE WANTING

... every morning and no morning at all—the frigate bird made of crepe paper & hung from the window of my daughter's classroom (precursor to lightning)—how to open & eat a pomegranate perfectly: the sound they make as storm-like & tempting—the hock of earth spit loose from the lawn mower: a different kind of scattering but still a scattering—the storm siren ready & wanting—the Pocomoke Sound ready & wanting to be gathered like a fever-struck child—a house where a little girl is taught what is right over what is pleasing: a new kind of categorical imperative—she thinks *if only I could cut out the part of me shaped like wanting*— wanting is wind shaped and tender fruit—the frigate bird beats the glass: it's papery song half-votive half-hymn—teaching my daughter how to open & eat pomegranates perfectly— precursor to wanting—& let's talk about how to be large in small spaces: synonym for hurricane —cargoes of cotton bales & dust covered fingers & hurricane lamps or: storms that are catalysts for inextinguishable light—my daughter's small body, her large hungers—the inevitable need for consuming: similitude of hurricane—a little girl's suddenly useless gray raincoat— extinguished light—a half dream precursor to a whole one—a little girl hauling bags of creosote: her abandoned checkerboard, her slow & careful casting—the idlest day, the tenderest eyelid, the body covered, the body hidden, the body emptied of wanting—the landscape's revision under the will of a storm—the body's revision under the will of a storm—a storm & its count- less multiples—its shape-shifting body—the things that are left: pomegranate not yet halved; my daughter not yet born; rain not yet swallowed; a half-girl trapped in a crape myrtle's branches. Gigi, I wonder, who the first birds flew home to.

MAJOR ARCANA 1: RANDY (PLAINFIELD, VT)

after Frances F. Denny

in meadows, a woman can look like a girl: wrinkled pockets,

a pendant upheld & backlit by her last year's close calls.

from here on out it's all about divination *&* liking blankets

that make noises (*Randy, there's a sound for you reaching*).

from here on out it's all about that ancillary pain & her wrists' slow-slightening

diameter. how she can be afraid of the dark too &

what's inside it (*your life like a picture that didn't turn out*).

how she saw a cloud in a baby (*its head a pale onion*) & not vice versa.

& what would *you* ask her? how she wound up in chamomile country

(*softening its clay-covered shoulders*), ready for her outlaw? why she wears that same

dust-colored dress & fancies the birds' more circular

prophecies (*as they bracelet the tree line*). or would you ask of your own

lost causes (*no yes or no answers*) with their fine-tooth

& ceaseless scratching? where all her life she's believed in the rings of trees

& the sadness of house-flowers, the jagged scrawl

of grocery-list-penmanship (*to feed you*). where all her life she's made the wind chime *(without glass)* & waited for some touch (*some perfect touch*)

to feed her.

ABANDONED SESTINA

I sat down to write a poem about god instead
wrote a poem about the dog

we saw hit by the Chrysler in May. *Such an un-May-like*
thing, you said. Who should die while the flowers

bloom? Everywhere, tussock was trembling. Looked like
fields of frostbitten hair. Looked like dead mice shot

on the floor of the kitchen. Sometimes, I give away food.
And sometimes I write letters to fake boyfriends

and sometimes when I stand beneath trees
I dream about graveyards for dogs that used to be gods

in the eyes of their children. Doesn't matter. This does:
in our backyard, often, I watch good gods shooting

arrows at bad ones. *Ouch*, says a new-struck god
and *why, oh why, did you do that?*

Overhearing this, I think, I have never felt
closer to god. I am struck by the effort to strike.

I am often asking and reading into this
act. Whereas you are cleaning

the blacktop of blood, chipping at diamonds of new
dog-red. Whereas sometimes I steal

the petty cash. And sometimes I waste
the mountain or avoid all the flowers.

And sometimes a Chrysler reminds me of angels
of death. Coming to carry the shot gods home

and the struck dogs back, our backyard a graveyard
of arrows and light. In the kitchen, I sat down to write.

A poem about the floor of the kitchen. Instead:
a poem about matter and diamonds of hair

flowers in the fingers of all our children,
not yet dead, not yet born, not yet bored by the blacktop—scrubbed

of its blood—and struck by stray arrows, points
of contact bringing short sparks of

light. Life. Flung by small gods who are trying to shoot
their way into largeness. Again, I think,

I have never been closer. What could I scrub out?
The gods? The blood? The eyes of my father remembering:

once there was a war that's still going. More than dogs died
in backyards that soon became graveyards, in

sometimes that soon became always and arrows that turned
into sharp blights of light in the sky: diamonds of dead flowers

struck. *Someday,*
no one will die in May, you said.

I, too, have considered surrender.

CRYPTID POEM

"The body must be heard." —Hélène Cixous

here comes hearsay: after bluebird; heresy after pines bow down to—thunder happens; this is hardly feasible sustenance, soundscape so capable of turning its own bed down—blood: blue & begging, relinquish, release, ready redness for dripping; light into ligature, moon into muscle— this strange wildness, that girl, bringing water to foxes—the space between fingers; the space between fingers pointing—skin thin & hardly becoming—drinks every river she swims in, blood part tributary; how soft her earlobes & traceable spine—the German word for poison is the English word for gift—the word for forgiveness is the sound for outrunning—her horse-dream: starving & girl dream: bodied not—horse is to girl as love is to wolf—her exile; her snow-pocked woods, new wet like white moon—season of doing—morning of listing; things to get away with:—orison to oracle & orator to orbit or else she forgets her own losing; or else she goes elsewhere—skinned open as a door—skin is to branch: pruned; woods so like habits: she grows into them—the night is when trees grow their tallest; there is sound for this also, her bones ricked & calling—a plum blooms come nightfall—she walks into this sacrifice

COURAGE THE COWARDLY DOG GOES OFF ON A TANGENT

Since December I've been putting my body back together. Hunting for loose screws in my pant legs. I'm told, *you're only just now getting around to it?* I've always crossed streets too slowly. Why should this be any different.

At night I climb up my skin with fingers. Say here is my forearm and here is my wrist. Wholly aware of what has been touched and what hasn't. The child in me asks where I keep the sadness. In my wild little chest? In my crooked little legs? In the places of touch.

As a girl, I kept a list of the things I'd become when I die: Stormcloud. Monolith. Coda. A bird suspended in unmeltable ice. These bodies maintain a distance. I.e., no one *likes* to touch ice. No one can force their way inside a storm. This body maintains a hesitance. Invasion vs. Discovery and other fine distinctions.

Since January I've been mixing up parts. The haunch of a dog. The mind of a planet. The lungs of a flightless bird. My human fingers dwindle like light. The only morning I woke without fear is four and a half years in the future and I'm told to believe this is beautiful. I've forgotten the taste of plums. I have bled in every ocean. I have touched many shoulders to see how they hold.

A possibility. Suppose I were the dog. Forgetting what my body feels like. Falling asleep pressed up against the water bowl, mistaking its scuffed white for a private moon. Today I ate a peach pit whole, spat it into the carpet and it bloomed a rabbit I went on to hunt. Miracle. Miracles can be just as tough to swallow. Much like bodies, miracles aren't always entirely beautiful.

Forsythia. A highly allergic frog. A part-time bee, part-time flower. A river rock. A blanket. Believable. A hill. A rolling, rolling hill.

No one buys me a thunder coat so I feel its rumble hitch ribs. What is beauty? What is body? Everything I have tried to replace stacks up like hollow eggs. Now and then it all feels a little alien. This desire to forget in forgiving. This desire to feel like a freshly washed pear. I talk into the crooks of my newly grown elbows. *Father,* I say. *Brother,* I say. *Mother: all I ask is to be loved as if I've just come home to you.*

I've just come home to me. Unbuttoning the unbuttonable parts of myself. Starting the mad scramble. I wonder if want is wantless: just a way to feel dead without dying. Or impossibly alive with unwound light. Fear is an expression of awe. I believe this. I am a blue-gold fish washed up on shore. I am learning to walk with new legs.

Let this be the place my garden grows. My hatchet splits. The neck of wood. Let this be my reptile hunger. My high-tide eyes. A house I decide to build. Most nights I fall asleep dreaming of something I almost said. Most nights happen. I wish there were an end of the earth I could drive to. Just to see what an edge looks like. Just to climb back from.

How many ways to say I miss? The old me. The old friend. The people I lost once. I always pray while I'm plugging in my phone so I'm not sure it counts. I cry every time I eat bread. Am suspicious of knobs on cabinets. I know if I outlive my anger, I will outlive the only part of me that feels large. I am against the sky. Enough has been said about it. The ground has uses also. And smallness too, I am learning.

I put on weather like a raincoat and decide to tell a story about foxes who outfox the vestigial memory. I have not yet realized there are no more ways to hide. There are more than moments to a life. There are more bodies yet undiscovered in the deeper parts of the water. In the deeper parts of the self.

I cross my skin like I cross the street. Slowly. With great deliberation. Tiny roads that stretch long distances compel me. I search them for evidence. Who has crossed here. Who has stayed here. Who lived to tell the story. In another life, I may have been considered. In another life, I may have learned sooner all the things I wanted to say before the moment passed for Saying.

A moment. When the sad story becomes a story about accepting its sadness. And suddenly turns pretty. A clipping of grass. A barely inflated rose. A soon-to-be drift of snow. Water seeks its own level. I seek it also.

ANYTHING WITH SKIN

Stapling the sky to my eyes if not for light,
for vastness. I go small in the eaves

of mountains. It's hard to tell if it's meant to be
this way. I go small in the face of apples also. Of drying

bars of soap. A field getting ready to weather. Anything with skin
that tears. Sewing the face of a former self

to my shoulder feels like a daily ritual. Something to press
my ear to when mostly I am knocking at sound

the way one tosses rocks at a branch of low-hanging fruit-
lessness. I like to think I'm full and don't need the meat

of a cageless heart. I like to think I contain.
And should I peel open, great rivers of future would startle

out. Surprised to see life so early. But I'm not involved
in the ways we forgive. Involved more in the way a deer

who's survived a wreck walks into the night afraid of
light's suddenness.

//
All night, lemons have dropped from the tree outside
my window. Outside me. Like revelations. Like rain.

When this wakes me, I imagine catastrophes:
the moon falling down like an earring. My father

on the floor, after stumbling—
such a rare thing for fathers to do.

A glass on the table divides my face
into diamonds of light. My eyes are the eyes

of an animal. My eyes are exactly what my eyes
shouldn't be.

//
The day I was invented, my mother's eyes shrunk,
it seemed, on her face. Trying to see inside me:

what could she contain? For years since, I've been making
eyes small. I consider this a value statement.

Here lies the girl difficult to discern. Here lies the girl
misanthropic. Here lies the girl who, as a girl,

once saw a deer flecked with blood in the grocery
store parking lot. Whose eyes were incredible lies.

Who limped all the way to the forest. And never
once thought to say goodbye.

I pretend I can buy my past lives in that store. A special
store where I'm boxed and shelved and glistening.

And can choose some story, some fate. Someone I loved
told me once:

You weren't invented, you were born. But I embody
a toiled figuration. I feel like a trinket. A lie.

//
A figure just under the skin of my arm. A bloom
at the corner of a mouth. A fly bent and broken

in glass. These are the supplies
of my dreams. I rarely transcend them.

The deer move in floods of light. They do not
ask me to follow, no matter how close I get.

I have failed in attempts to be animal. After all,
I cannot sit through a hurricane

without tracing my own kneecaps. Thinking
who's touched them. I wonder how capable.

I wonder how hard one must push on glass
to break it. On skin. At the drugstore,

I ran into an old friend who told me the
story of her lightness. *It's a fabrication*,

she confessed. And like everything else,
it wanes, weakens, strengthens.

//
While elsewhere, weeks collect
in placid lulls. The rain fails

every day. Today,
a deer emerges with exactly seven

spots. Can walk within hours
of being born.

//

I'm asked what my spirit animal is.
I choose a fish and am asked, *what,*

no deer? I say I want to believe
I don't need to be a part of each thing

that I love when, really, I'm afraid
of love. Its fine and skittish skin.

I could never contain it.
I wonder my animal fear. Is it this?

I think of divination. How, once,
the scapulae of deer were used to find

answers. When real pain
is in the asking. I wonder

each animal's prayer. If saying *I need you*
counts as a prayer.

//

Today, I will remember the fruit
pits I collected and stored as a girl. Imagining

they were the lost hearts of all my dead
animals. A rabbit in the remnant of a peach,

a bird, a dog. The pruned lines of
something to trace and to hold. Here lies the pit

you could swallow. Contain. They are building
a greenhouse at the motel down the street. They

are braiding vines like green fingers to glass.
I imagine inside, it is dark. With all that leafy

curtain. I imagine inside, it is almost hard to breathe.
There is so much ready air. Will the fruit come

in there? Bear a pit to smuggle in the dark.
In my hold, days go on with more asking.

A comforting and bittersweet
regularity.

//
The field, from my window, blooms
with deer. Their heads suspended

to study the distance. They look away,
I think. Never at what's in front of them.

I tell them I forgive
them now because I know,

someday,
I will mean it.

FIELD NOTES

The rules: in the dream, you are thin as cursive. In the cursive, you are lettering want. Still as an X, you have also learned irrelevance. Disuse. The photo of your mother at a beach. Her lookable body. The blood on the chair that looks like an ending. The ending that looks like a soft place to land. In the dream, you will notice the hedges. The way the trees, on the island, are shaped by the wind: their necks twisted back like little girls & misery: put out of. In the misery, you will climb like a tree. Here is the steadying arm. Here is the dream, washing her hair in the river. This is the law of the wild: the river doles out favors. When you learn to ask, you learn to swim. When you learn to forgive, you learn to swim away.

Cutting a flat rock into sheets of sharp, listening to the way a shaving almost sounds like a bell. Trying to use one's hands. My brother carries buckets of water long distances & never cowers. I have not yet learned this persistence. Today I read about the traces of a hurricane: hundreds of horses, dead by letting. Swarms of mosquitoes gathering. Today I wrote a letter and it felt some same draw of blood. Because I am lonely, I am always shying away from the mirror.

My grandmother told me once, all girls grow up to be women who know how to let their fingers dry. Plucking the stem from a cherry, she makes me a reprimand. Tells me I am crooked in my want. Then again, I *have* lied. There was never a cherry. My grandmother told me: all girls grow up to be women who know how to lie.

Today they found a body in the river, tangled up like cursive. We dragged on the news like smoke. Yet another woman lost. I think about the way I never told my mother of the second man to touch me without asking. In fact, I never told anyone. But for years after, I'm said to have said in my sleep *where did I put the knife?* When I have headaches, I bear them. Or else, I take tiny pills I imagine are Christmas lights. I am afraid of Christmas. I am not afraid of dreams. My grandmother told me once: all girls grow up to be women and I lied: in my sleep, I never say a word. I imagine I swallow that light.

In dreams, I imagine myself giving things away. In dreams, I walk into that river. Saying what I'm saying now: here. I am telling *you.* Because I am lonely, I am always looking for signs.

EKPHRASTIC POEM OF HOLLY'S BROWN LOCKET
PAINT SWATCH, OR: THINGS THAT ARE LOST TO ME

Holly, I never knew: what picture you kept there, what wildness got lost. Was it Shawn in the water? With his fingers new and clean. Did those veins in his forearms rise the way roots rise: just there beneath the earth. And how far does honey travel from the jar? From the mouth. Far as a switchblade? As wetflesh or night receding? I was never much for nightshade. Never found the earth all that receivable. But some nights trace the hollow of my neck for a locket that could fall there: big as a thumb pressing down wholeness. Wholeness feels like a stone swallowed—there are tougher stones to swallow. But you know that don't you, Holly? You cast light bright as the color of an untraced photograph. Too much to look at. You are so far from the earth you bleed raincloud. When he swam for you, he swallowed two quarts of the ocean and swelled with it. All his cyclical softness. All his urgency yours. Holly: you never wanted to watch the storms coming. Only ever saw midnight as a locket with a broken chain: dangling, just about to fall. I was too young to think about trespass. I was too young to worry about beauty. How some people grow up to feel trapped in an ocean.

HARVEST WRECKAGE

mouth light and choose   tuned
    weather—blackberries spill
their   unbled   clean—

march each harvest out—keep
      going—back:

light. litany
.   another
you.

DREAM IN WHICH MY BODY IS A SNOWSTORM

and doesn't make anyone cold. If I fell I would fall
in state-shaped flakes. One for every place my body
lingered. One for every little bit of light I stole
and kept. No cars startless. No tangled-up roadways. Neck
becoming mountain of drift; foot becoming fierce kicking
eddies. Heat would not melt me. Hands would not help
me undo. Blanketing softly. Whimsy not pretend.
Dream in which my body is a snowstorm and the storm says
a purpose in falling

SIMULTANEITY STUDY, OR: WHAT PRAYERS DO

Our father is reciting Our Fathers. We are listening but getting the words wrong.
Winter: looks like the inside of an ashtray. The ashtray: split

like the seam of a lip. Houses, everywhere, are full of things we've thought of throwing.
Throwing at someone we loved. Our father: cycling the last *daily bread*

sounding like *daily dead*. Give us our daily dead and forgive us our
smashed glasses—we threw them. We loved so much we thought we were beautiful.

Remember? When deliverance was a coaster in the East? When this was the furthest to fall?
Remember? When prayers were all that belonged to our father? Our father

singing with Hafez. And his voice doesn't sound like a prayer. And his voice doesn't sound
like *so many dead*. So we save him. Or we judge him. For his many ways of staying

on his knees. We don't tell him about the boys in school. Who press their bodies
on our pants without asking. Who say *Hail Mary* when they rain their hard hands

down. *We are loved like a winter storm* we think. We get good at the prayer-like
lies. Remember the dentist in sixth grade? Who said we should lie about our name?

Say it's anything but Arab. Our father unknowing, in the waiting room, trenching
the spine of a book. *Deliver us or he will*... as in: what man won't want to

tell you how to save yourself. When our father gave us the talk about leaving
—just: *sometimes you have to*—we thought he

looked the way God must have looked once. Uncertain.
Do I keep going filing the light in his eyes.

So we get good at the prayer-like secrets. We don't tell and *don't tell*. We Hail
Mary for the locks on bathroom doors.

And in eighth grade, we bury the dog with bare and bearable
hands. Uncertain what prayers do—

—and leave us knots in two split nations—the dogwood throwing

her house on us. We are loved, we are bruised, we are living
our two different lives. Somewhere, someone is throwing a carefully loved

book. Finding a new way to make love
mark. Our father tells a story about replanting the trees. How, overnight,

their twisted arms reach further and further. And for a moment our father
—whose art is in heaven—is talking about us. How even,

in the dark, we grow.

THINGS BENEATH THE SKY

what gray knows of beauty
small things lost in tight
rivers—my jars all have uses

this light is less practical
than that. i remember the hospital.
though these wings are no—

no. too easy. things beneath the sky:
their gladness? i call *easy, too easy, too wrong.*
i throw the thick rules down:

apple. and naked. mother unskinning
her shoulder from my shoulder. both of us
touched once.

i am mostly a part of my keeping—
eurydice, maybe, made a choice.
i have punished my blue jays

also. i have held close my wildness
and turned it against them with
enough twisting, leaves

at the pane turn into a locust.
as in: plague of. with enough
urging my throat spits up seeds.

not for nothing,
they won't grow 'til morning.
their fruit will bite sharp as

an answer. *where* they asked
did he touch you? what gray
knows of beauty: those bookends.

where the river goes down in its
searching. where i swim in the
answers of lowness.

things beneath the sky roar back
in their land thrall. i will learn
to root my mark in it.

EKPHRASTIC POEM OF SCANDINAVIA-BLUE PAINT
SWATCH, OR: (THINGS THAT ARE NAKED)

We got off the ark. It was snowing. Naked as April. It was April. Wide awake at the summit. Creating space: not easy. You lifted color, instruction, the wholeness of bread. My spine ran with heat like the L charging down its track. Heat can be blue. This blue even. Fruit flies gathered on the rim of the horse's blind eye. Do they mistake him for soft berries? *Blue*berries. We blind eye to blue just because nothing is totally so. We break the grid by scrubbing. I scar long as a centipede & new skin grown over. Even castles have cobwebs. Even arks have escape routes. This blue is the blue of all the skin can hold. This snow is the snow of my last wildness. Years after the lake was last useful to me. We are against the sky & its ways of describing. Full up of great starts to other people's stories. Holding a hand close to my eye feels like being washed away. & there is no color in that. There are many colors in that. & the ark is not waiting. Anymore. This is that gone-ness in color. These are the hard sounds that fling forward. & truth is this is how you become full. There are rules for midnight's colors: none of this softness though another kind of softness, quiet as an errant prayer. *I am mostly a part of my keeping* I say. *Have we looked long enough to start walking?* you ask. I run my hands down in the soft. I feel like a little spy pulling that last glimpse upward. This color becoming that color like the last good getaways. Truth is my hands feel more held when the water runs through them

CORIOLIS

      Say the stovetop. Say the wet March trudged through.
Say I am *just* and I am *only* and I am trying to cup sandstorms
in two spare palms. Say it wasn't a lie and it wasn't made up. And
the bridge froze over because it's just what bridges do. Say you can find
a part of me in every now-asleep storm. Say sun was never a bandage
and Greyhound never had a bus with enough gas and the getting was
never all that good but we smiled anyway.

     *

      What we make of the beloved. Those hands twisted
in the lamplight. Fun fact: I've never proven anyone wrong. Which was
meant to be funny. What we try to rub warm with light. What I tried housing
to keep my darkness company. I swallowed whole rivers. My veins are part
tributary. What recollects there. Every now and then I go down
to the river and stay there. What truth is truer than those that start with wanting.
I could never tell you anything useful. Even the lies have no matter. What it takes
to be restless. What I often decide, probing home like an electric bill you thought
was a love letter. I have never been colder. I have never been queen here.

     *

      Say filament frilled. Say I spent years wondering what to do with my hands.
So I spent a year getting it wrong. Seeing a ghost in every
upturned cup. Every moth trapped. The wettest roses and the falsest warmths.
Say I pushed my hands into the mud and expected to find minnows. Say it was never
supposed to be another way.

     *

Take the wild and its dead kingdoms. Take the opossum I watched
my father kill. And Shouri the tiger, killed for her wander. Take my brother's
wide brown eyes, and a ghost's gentle thumbs. Say it could be used. I am with
wind's starstruck fractures. I like things scattered also. Say this was all about that.
Was all about learning to murmur. Say I had any kind of idea about damage and its
uses. Say I wanted to live in the weedbed. Say I was figuring out how to
plant a storm in every little loss there was. To wreck it but also to lift it. To bare.

     *

Ghost dreams: where my skin is full grocery bags. Where this thumb burns
a hole. Where I am unkind to the spines of books. Leave channels deep enough
to cup matchsticks. Where I radiator limb and search for an angel.
Where I remember my father: pruning roses.
Eclipsing the eye of a gun.

     *

Say you only love home when it's rain-soaked. Take the rain, for example.
Now that's power. All my watches stop clicking. All my funeral clothes wear
down, turn from black to gray, to no color in particular. What if there was a word
that described every doorway that ever felt empty. Every restless night spent trying
to find some glimpse of your family in a left-behind shirt. Once I left a shirt in a hotel
in Poughkeepsie. Some remnant that was never that precious. Some shape that survived
me when I was trying to be survived. Every time someone says my name it surprises me.
I drink every river I swim in. I learned the word *holding* in fourteen different languages.
Here I thought that would make a difference.

     *

Here a voice left like paper blown. On voicemail, a cousin. *I am bringing home milk.*
I sat with his New Wife. They showed us pictures of the car, its body as lifeless. Or more so.
Fender strung out like waves. Hear its great twisting? The phantom nearness. The body full
up of home-soon and no guardrails, blacktop pocked with new white like wet
skin. Milk carton open as an eggshell split on the lip of my counter. Where years earlier
I had told him not to touch my scar. *I burned it* I said. Hear the explanation? Like I was tired
of being marked.

*

Take the ghost. Who sturdily is. Dreaming of tiger traps and milk-
weed. Say I said I made it up in an act of contrition. As if story could stop
a death. Say every night since I have dreamt of fenceless winters. Woke to find
it was no blue dream. Take the dream. Take that image doled out in each
long, trembling road. As if taking meant keeping. As if missing was something new.

*

Wonder where grief goes after. In the bone. In the gold bands of wheat stalks tipped
mountainwards. Say it's okay to not be who I was. Say my brother was
old mountain. And each time a shadow stretched it was his tidy little yawn.
Say my family: new ocean, to which every good thing is carried. Wonder if I
press my ear to a gull will I hear ocean speak back. Wonder if each time I dream, I am
learning to say goodbye.

COURAGE THE COWARDLY DOG ANNOUNCES HIS RETIREMENT

"I am human therefore nothing human is alien to me." —The Self-Tormentor, Terence

hum is reef
man is no more a moor to tie
a gale to

anymore i am lien to fog
i am fig-intimate
no hinge to hem

no hail to not ignore
no grief i fail to note
no goat ignoring horn

or horn ignoring fame
of another
name

the fang is not alien to me
nor the fog
nor the fume of time's mourning

no more—no more
life of no resting
no more fear for muriel

mourning is not all human
nor home *all* human—no more
groan torn from throat—no more one hum:

hum is reef
i am floating on its
great gait as figment

i am all fruit tree
i am true truth that
        nothing is ever all gone.

SUPPLIES FOR A QUICK MIGRATION

Hard heart or hardable. Water walking shoes. Rope, river, raft. Ladder and lasso,
lychee or image of. Lightable fires. Your latchable dreams. Some small magic. Disposable
magic. Disclosed hunger. Willingness to budge. To be desolate. To be made into. In two.
One heart of you here one self completely indiscernible. A song to bruise you. A bush
to flame. A metaled cold for any softness left. Leavable histories. Room for an urging
hunger. Whoever will follow. Closeable eyes to those who will not. A pencil, or not. A knife
or a knot. To grow. A small seed to sow into a slightly less small seed. An eye for exceptions.
Acceptance or lack of. A honed ear to places where home-sounds sneak through.
The thing is, your body becomes you. Thing is, there is no such place
as the end of you.

CRYPTID POEM // VICTIM IMPACT STATEMENT

1.
Sounds of men saying yes.
Carpets with footprints broken in.

"Good girl" says the Muse:
she was good once too.

I have answers to questions
no one asks anymore—

it's not the saddest story in the world.
But at least it's a story.

It's in fashion to be inexcusable: to have
a gown that opens easily. Close your eyes

and dream of a handless world. All the
harder to grab you. All the turn

in a phrase. When I was young
all I wanted was a double door.

How things change. Now I want
a door that can't open. This started

off a funny poem. Isn't that funny?

2.
Picking up trash in the garden.
Happy happy family.

Two young lovers walking up a hill.
Will he like her hands? Or will he

only touch her hair to move it?

3.
Hands that feel like beginnings.
Hands that are actually endings.

Every time I strike a match,
I imagine being put to bed.

My father pulls the blanket over.
His hands are impossible walls.

I think of all I can't tell him about
the man down the street.

How his hands pulled the bedsheet
down. How, in dreams, he replaces my father.

I know what it feels like to be held.
But also know what it is

to be touched.

4.
Hand me a good little lie.
I can use what I cannot believe.

5.
Midas must have lived quite the life.
Afraid to touch anyone he loved.

The lake-line was faint as a heartbeat.
I walked my way towards the heartbeat
then stopped. How many ways to say
I miss and keep missing.
I remembered the hole in your sweater.
I imagined a fingertip's worth of skin.
I ate bread like it was mercy.
I hated you. I hated you less and less
as the seconds passed until I never hated you.
This is grief's best card trick:
showing you love is what
prayers are. I built a house. Where
the windows never
close and the doorways
never empty. I stopped.
I did work. I did work that made
me hurt more and more and
then less and less. I ate the whole hearts
of lemons that filled me with
electricity.
I thought *this is how floods feel.*
I was glad to be full of a feeling for
something other than you.
I blew out the candles and wiped down
the counters. I watched a crow
circle that hollow valley. I watched
the day go down to rest
and I let it.
For once, I thought,
let this time be gentle.
I traced a rail line on the map,
imagined there: a shoulder.
I loved you so I tried to build you.
And then I emptied all
the drawers. I bought new sheets

Some days I feel like that. That my touching
is usurped by touch. The history

of traces. But Midas isn't known for his
fear. Fear isn't known as

expression of awe.

6.
Sounds of the Muse coming back.
Sounds of the mice in the attic.

When I dream of myself, my mouth
blooms many hands. They reach in all

shapes and directions. I am trying to forgive
without thinking. Maybe this

is entirely the point.

7.
Today, everyone was holding hands.
All cities, even small ones, feel large to me.

When I sit by the harbor,
I can almost feel beautiful.

8.
The Muse says *Darling*.
You have told him this.

INVENTORY

after Ted Hughes's thirty writing prompts for his daughter Frieda

(17) obstacles to spying on my neighbors in the early hours; the bird's-eye view of our city, grape-like and breaking (18) pairs of eyes receiving these final weights goodnight and crowing (19) yards in which I've felt your arm like branch; its quiet and receding forgiveness—its enveloping rain (20) houses dark with geometry books—the wink of fire cauterizing the gentle pad of two new foxes in the undergrowth outside, their backs white and wet with ice (21) times they said to take it easy now, *these things happen in January* (22) different occasions for mourning you in the grocery store, the canned peas parting curtain and the screeching music this makes (23) words and pauses before intermission, the head of the protagonist lopped off and dripping on its valiant stand, soliloquy for us and the mournful understudy who knows he could *die better* (24) times the stem was stepped on before bending fully at the neck (25) beginnings of my thoughts of you—forgetting would be easier? (26) places where my mother lost me as a child in the crooked elbow of the hiking trail (27) seasons of forgetting what milk tastes like: a meteorological sensation (28) people sleeping in trees for different reasons (29) notes of me turning the page of the dictionary trying not to look at you—the sharp spine of almost-silence (30) doctors that have been kept away; they reappear pursuing ornithology—*Lipoma. Mantle. Sapiens. Accipitridae.*

(1) time we missed the bus and walked for hours in the wheatgrass (2) nods from the passenger to the left, on the plane, wondering who would pick me up at the airport (3) bags of wood shavings for pet; trying to fill the void of you (4) moves ahead of you closing the windows and turning the thermostat down (5) taxidermists' opinions that there is no point in keeping you from sailing off (7) animals I tried to nurse back to health—tired of letting things die (6) animals I could not save and what to do with their bodies afterward (8) people who warned me I've a habit of wounding myself (9) pieces of mail addressed to other people, your wordlessness a weight more than paper (10) concussed fractals—earth breaking for weed like bone (12) drops of laudanum on my hungry tongue and your gentle leaving (13) seconds of bravery, your head turned responding to that first *hello* (14) pivotal moments you forgot to wish me goodnight (15) months in recovery—therapy bird I saved at the window with a mouth of rain and crash-landing manuals (16) hours in the house, closing you in boxes, buying my ticket out of this empty place.

(11) spots of mold in your bathroom—I wash away with snow

I'm trying to prove to God why I need a getaway car
but it's hard to quantify suffering to God without
feeling like I'll be punished for it. So, I suppose:
getaway cars

*

are the ghosts of everything I didn't prove and
God is a fear of punishment and punishment is an
inability to number the things that need escaping:
suffering, the Doomsday Clock in Union Square, God,
punishment, my unbreakable heart and its many
ways of, still, breaking.

*

I'm trying to break the right way. The way God broke
the ocean with footsteps. The way cars cut a darkness
with headlights, slice the highway like ghosts in my
apartment as soon as I turn the lights off. Trying to
prove: things linger. Whether you can name them or
not. The getting's not always good in the getaway,
more often than not: it's suffering through the heart's
slow yearn for thread

*

capable of sewing its split seams and missing light.
I'm trying to prove to God that their punishment is
redundant when I'm so good at punishing myself. The
way I still lick envelopes. The way I continue to live in

an apartment with cold spots. The way I drive in the
dark without headlights, sometimes, when I feel like
seeing a ghost.

*

But often I've mistaken Jesus for God and I worry I'll
be punished for it. I.e., *God* never broke the water:
God broke angels into humans and earth into oceans
of ghosts and ghosts into the hearts of people who
never learned to feel fear, to linger in fear, to notice
that punishment is just another way of saying *do
better* and doing better is just another way of getting
in a car and driving home instead. Proof

*

is antithetical to God. So I've been told. The way cars
can't be numbered on the highway without crashing
into light. I'm trying not to crash into light. But I'm
worried I'll be punished for it. Because if I don't crash
into light, does that mean I have chosen the dark?
I suppose dark capable.

*

Of lingering in the split seams of my apartment.
Of lingering in the split seams of God? I suppose I'll
be punished for that. For saying God's light can get
away in a car and drive to Union Square to tamper
with the Doomsday Clock. To say, here: let me split
the time into oceans of *do better.* Let me feel fear like
a human who has turned into an apartment filled
with ghosts.

*

Filled with thread that can't bear its own tension,
tension that can't prove holding worth it. I am trying
to be worth a getaway. I am trying to quantify the
heart's slow yearn for stasis, stasis which

*

can only be found by driving the highway with
lights trained on the windows of apartments filled
with dark. Saying *do better.* Let something linger.
Let God understand the lights off and the ghosts
understand, through the cars, what it means to move
on. I'm trying to move on. On into the split seams
of my lingering. Lingering in the time spent missing
the light.

*

On the time spent trying to prove: I am not breaking.
I am growing a space for a ghost's God to name my
slow yearn for home. My slow yearn for thread that
can draw old fear to new stillness

EAVESDROPPING

1. What water said about loss:
His body is a small tributary. And a mostly blue
planet. Fig suspended in the sad remnants of a river.
Though sometimes lagoonal, more often a wound built in the morning
when every light looks winter.

2. What loss said back:
I trust Him to know but also I call Him
equally fathomless—real beauty coming in the way
people gather in droughts. The bleachy moon
over towns abandoned by water—great husks of crop
petrified like the parts of an engine. Smothered in sand.
Asking for His trim, unending gaze—graceless as a moment feels
tenseless, a tiny aperture: the reasons why there's more
black in the lake than blue.

3. What I told water:
I want a single word for complex acts
like forgiveness and going. Like your ice blue fingers
tipping balut toward the mouth—a mottled body soft
when swallowed. I want time compressed on the surface
of a meager lake: how it freezes so easy yet it doesn't feel
like cheating. I want less ice from your skin
than a tender flake torn from a great storm & landing soft here.

4. What I told loss:
Show me how to thumb the valleys of my ribs for air.
How to gut an errant fish with no waste, make an altar
from its bones. How to love in the service of loneliness, use
what I'm given. Teach me how a cloud shoulders a storm. It shouldn't hold
but it does and I don't know why.

5. What water said back:
I have answered in hurricanes. In small
waterfalls and the sounds of ice cleaving. In teaching you how
to float on your back like a loose orchid.

6. What I looked for in loss, and found only in water:
A body losing volume. My ear pressed to the chest
of a stranger—searching for sound, finding only an unmoved sycamore
—a shell in a shell where the ocean drank back its moan.

7. What loss said back to me: Imagine a lake that swallows snow
and does not turn white. Says:
every time I love you
it surprises me.

SOLILOQUY

for J.

I went like a kid to the valley.
I blew up the gray balloons.
I gave my skies boundaries:
they scarred in the middle like stomachs.
I broke like a little grape. I gave in and thought
at least I'm still giving. I untied
the shoes of a man I wanted more from.
I slept in the attic with matches.
I pulled the gristle from the pan. I ate
from the back of the icebox:
the dried leaves and little grapes.
I thought *I am wild*
and *I am getting older.*
The streets looked doused in milk.
I wanted to drink from them.
But not really: I wanted to skate on them.
All the way towards Georgia
to say goodbye to you. I sat on the stairs
and counted my knuckles. I blew
blue rings of smoke in the ashen
morning light. I asked an angel
to help with my laundry. *It will be*
like a game I promised. Where I take
the time to tidy. In the mirror,
I looked like the kid in the raincoat.
For a moment
I wanted to grow orchids.
I walked along the fenceline. I made a list
of griefs. And thought *this must be*
what prayers are.
The horses ate and kept eating.

and spread them out
like acres. I gave my anger to the birds.
I am wild I said.
I almost believed it and thought
at least I am almost believing.
I built another house. I filled it
with everything that stopped hurting.
I thought, *this is what grief*
reveals: that love is full of mistakes.
In the house I built a chair
I knew, someday, I wouldn't need.

I pulled the chair by the bed
should I wake to find you'd come

TO GRIEF, WITHOUT ASKING

You indiscrete son, you bird-like sun, you ellipsis, you waver and I come to a gulley, wade in the gulley, go to the woman next door and ask for a disaster. To spread the disaster down my cold and waiting hands. I want to see it, feel its papery strength— paper that could hold a word, could hold this gold failure to breathe. The woman lost her husband, could not find him in the park, found him in the illness—a triptych of adenoma. You go where you want without asking, don't you, little sparrow? She could not heal me the way she needed healing, we were gone to the grayed-out gulf—a dream? A god. Dead as a goat in the valley from the virus of you— worms scavenged him, we asked for a blanket to cover his tiny feet. I could name you like a gimmick, I could feed a piece of the storm back to you. We could praise you, graphite tenement, could redefine your arrows and gross curves. We went to the source, the woman and I, were ready to cure you. The goslings in the park were a languid few, were you there? Did you go, again, without asking? We could not cure you, that is all there is to say. It's just anger, as in deep or caused by the self or another, as in to say the hardship was the folklore. It seemed to bloom a quiet engine. What is the difference in loneliness? The antonym for bison or an unspecific noun? You ephemeral feeling, will you stay this time? I do not want or need your pity, I will soldier you away. But come into the room. Hand me a hurricane. I want to see what you're offering.

The "Disintegration Loop" series borrows its titles and inspiration from William Basinski's "Disintegration Loops."

"Poem That Starts with the Sound of Andy Warhol Eating a Cheeseburger" makes reference to the 1982 film *66 Scenes from America* by Jørgen Leth.

"Shadhavar" makes reference to a mythical character from ancient Muslim bestiaries. The creature's horns, when played on one side, produce a beautiful and happy sound. When played on the other side, the music can cause listeners to weep in sadness. In literature, these horns are often gifted to kings and noblemen.

"Autobiography As a Headless Girl" borrows the phrase "Headless girl" from Rita Dove's "Party Dress for a First Born."

"Cryptid Poem" borrows the phrase "the bug collector" from Hayley Heynderickx's "The Bug Collector."

"Aphantasia" refers to the inability to form mental images of objects that are not present.

"(21) // Victim Impact Statement" and "Inventory" make use of Ted Hughes's thirty writing prompts for his daughter Frieda Hughes, accessed via Emory University's Rose Library and rare manuscript archive.

"Autopsy" references the 2019 CNN article "A Lioness Ate Her Newborn Cubs Three Days After Giving Birth at a German Zoo."

"Where Have You Gone, Connie Converse" makes reference to the Connie Converse song "How Sad, How Lovely."

"Major Arcana 2: The Instruments" and "Major Arcana 1: Randy (Plainfield, VT)" are based off Frances F. Denny's photo series "Major Arcana: Witches in America."

"Reimagining the Interrogation of Betty Hill" takes questions from the PBS "Kidnapped by UFOs?" (*NOVA*) transcript.

"Cryptid Poem" takes the Hélène Cixous quote from *The Laugh of the Medusa*.

The "Courage the Cowardly Dog" poems make reference to the 1999–2002 Cartoon Network show *Courage the Cowardly Dog*.

"Simultaneity Study, or: What Prayers Do" borrows language from the Lord's Prayer.

"Things beneath the Sky" takes its title from John Ashbery's "Syringa."

"Coriolis" references Shouri, an Amur tiger mauled by two other tigers at Longleat Safari Park after a gate was left open between pens.